THE INGENIC

Other books by the Author

The Ninja and the Diplomat (volume 2 of The Chinese Spymaster), forthcoming September, 2015.

Agamemnon Must Die, a retelling of Aeschylus' Oresteia, 2014.

The Ingenious Judge Dee, a Play, 2014.

The Chinese Spymaster (volume 1, Operation Kashgar), 2013.

Heaven is High and the Emperor Far Away, A Play, adapted from "Teahouse," by Lao She (Shu Qingchun, 1899-1966) 2011.

The Battle of Chibi, selections translated from the "Romance of the Three Kingdoms" (by Luo Guanzhong, ca. 1400), 2010.

THE INGENIOUS JUDGE DEE, a Play

(Adapted from *The Celebrated Cases of Judge Dee*, an 18th century Chinese "detective novel," translated in 1949 by Robert van Gulik)

By

HOCK G. TJOA

Inquiries regarding performance rights may be sent to
tjoa.books@gmail.com.

CAST OF CHARACTERS

In order of appearance

JUDGE DEE, 40. A shrewd and energetic, even athletic man, he is a magistrate in a small county and has earned a reputation for his ingenious investigations into serious crimes.

BAILIFF, 45. A servant of the Court at Six Mile Village.

INSPECTOR HONG, 45. Formerly head servant in JUDGE DEE's family household, is now his senior investigator.

IMPERIAL CENSOR, 50. In disguise.

CLERK 1 and 2, non-speaking parts.

CHAO, 20-ish. Previously an outlaw, he was recruited by Judge Dee to be an investigator. He is alert and energetic.

MA, 20-ish. A friend of Chao's recruited at the same time.

TAO, 25. Previously a con artist and cat burglar, the Judge recruited her to be an investigator.

JAILER, a non-speaking part.

<u>Characters in the Case of the Double Homicide</u>

CONSTABLE PANG, a "good old boy" sheriff who is lazy, especially if it involves thinking.

INNKEEPER GONG, an older man who has built up his inn-keeping business by tenacity and scrimping and saving.

SHAO, 30. An itinerant silk merchant who is in love.

1

Characters in the Case of the Reluctant Corpse

GRAVE-DIGGER, an "old" man in his 50s.

MOTHER BEE, an "old" woman about 50 years old, mother of the deceased.

CHEN, 25. The deceased's best friend.

WIDOW BEE, 25. A beautiful woman, she commits murder to climb up the social ladder.

GRANDDAUGHTER BEE, 5.

YOUNG SU, 20s. Handsome, wealthy, of high social standing, flirt.

Characters in the Case of the Poisoned Bride

WIDOW LEE, 45. Mother of the Poisoned Bride.

YOUNG HUA, early 20s. The Bridegroom.

An ellipsis in speech indicates a pause, while "[*beat*]" denotes both a pause and something of a pivot in the direction or plane of the speech.

ACT I, Scene 1

(Courtroom of JUDGE DEE, the Magistrate of a small county in China around 700 AD. The setting is intended to give a rural and premodern feel but there is no attempt at historical accuracy.

The Courtroom is in Six Mile Village. As is the custom in ancient China, the Magistrate acts as investigator, prosecutor, and judge. The scene opens with the BAILIFF standing at the Center Rear. CONSTABLE PANG, and INNKEEPER GONG stand facing him. Two others sit to the Bailiff's left in the shadows, INSPECTOR HONG, chief of the investigators for JUDGE DEE, and an IMPERIAL CENSOR in disguise. Censors respond to allegations of improper behavior on the part of Imperial officers such as Judge Dee. Two clerks sit in front of the Bailiff to his right and transcribe the proceedings.)

BAILIFF: The Court of the Honorable Judge Dee is now in session. All rise! *(Everyone onstage stands.)* Welcome to the first of our hearings in the sixth month of the sixth year of the reign of the Emperor Rui Zong. *[=690 A.D.]*

(JUDGE DEE enters from CENTER LEFT and sits in front of the Bailiff facing the audience. CONSTABLE PANG and INNKEEPER GONG stand facing him. As the JUDGE sits, so do the others.)

JUDGE DEE: These hearings are ordered by the Imperial Court to address matters of concern to the people. Sometimes they are about missing chickens or cows. Occasionally, they are more serious. The

3

Court has sent me here to deal with all the issues troubling the people of this neighborhood. I understand that today there are two complaints: a most serious accusation of a double homicide and a counter-complaint of harassment. Constable Pang you first, please.

CONSTABLE PANG: (W*ith a swagger.*) Thank you, Your Honor. Two nights ago, a couple of silk merchants registered at the Inn owned by Innkeeper Gong. It is a respectable inn, popular with the locals. But the following day, I found two bodies a short distance from the Inn and also learned that the two guests at the Inn are no longer there.

INNKEEPER GONG (*rises agitatedly*): But…

JUDGE DEE (*firmly*): Please wait your turn, Innkeeper Gong.

CONSTABLE PANG: I therefore accuse Innkeeper Gong of murdering his two guests and stealing their goods.

(*Gasps and murmurs in the chamber.*)

JUDGE DEE: A double homicide! This is very serious. (*Beat.*) Is that all, Constable Pang?

CONSTABLE PANG (*"ain't-my-job" clueless, manner*): All?

JUDGE DEE (*in the tone of a strict uncle addressing a child, firmly but not rushing*): Yes, "all." Have you found witnesses to the murders? …Do you know what weapons were used? Have these been found? …Can the weapons be linked in any way to the Innkeeper? …Do you know if the goods are still with him? …Have you any evidence that the two bodies are those of the guests at the Inn? (*Stands and leans towards the Constable*) Do I need to go on?

CONSTABLE PANG (*Beat. The Constable is flummoxed but recovers): Er … I … I have full confidence that Your Honor will uncover all this.

4

JUDGE DEE (*sits and says severely*): I will get to the bottom of this, Constable. But you might have tried to find answers to some of these questions before accusing anyone of killing two men. (*Shakes his head.*) Innkeeper, you have a complaint, I believe.

(*The Constable sits as the Innkeeper rises to speak.*)

INNKEEPER GONG: Thank you, Your Honor. I accuse Constable Pang of harassing me and my establishment. He and his companions have often come, expecting their bills to be waived or paid for with only a token sum.

JUDGE DEE: How often have they done this?

INNKEEPER GONG: Once or twice a week. Sometimes they get drunk and rowdy and break furniture.

CONSTABLE PANG (*stands up to interject*): We have always paid for any damage!

JUDGE DEE (*icily*): Thank you Constable. (*The Constable sits.*) It is nice to have my questions anticipated by your answers, but if you don't mind, I'd like to ask my questions before you answer them ... Innkeeper, it is customary for establishments like yours to ... "do favors" for regular customers, is it not?

INNKEEPER GONG (*agitatedly*): Yes, but not all the time!

JUDGE DEE: Hm, what do you think is proper?

INNKEEPER GONG: Once a year.

JUDGE DEE (*stares at the Innkeeper and shakes his head*): I see; I believe that, at the MINIMUM, shops give their regular customers a treat during the Spring Festival celebrations. That's once a year. Many do so once or twice a month in addition—to keep relationships friendly. (*Taps his fingers on his desk.*) Anyway, I do not intend to tell you how to run your business. Do you acknowledge that there were two men who registered as guests at your inn?

INNKEEPER GONG: Yes, Your Honor. Their names were Lu and Shao. They said they were silk merchants on their way to the city. They asked if we could store their carts with their goods and they paid for their rooms and the storage for one night.

JUDGE DEE: Did you see them leave the next day?

INNKEEPER GONG: Not personally. I have a steward on the early morning shift. He informed me that they left very early the next morning.

JUDGE DEE (*turns to the Constable*): Constable, where did you find the bodies?

CONSTABLE PANG (*stands*): On the road to the city.

JUDGE DEE: Innkeeper, have you seen the bodies?

INNKEEPER GONG: No, Your Honor.

JUDGE DEE: You will have to go with Inspector Hong. Please see if you can identify the bodies. I caution you not to leave the village. Inspector, before you leave, bring your colleagues here. We must begin the investigation immediately, but I would like a word with you and your team. At least one murderer is on the loose.

BAILIFF: The Court of the Honorable Judge Dee is now adjourned. All rise!

(*Lights fade to black as all leave. A spot shows the BAILIFF approaching the IMPERIAL CENSOR who reveals an insignia to him. The BAILIFF puts his right fist on his heart and tries to get to his knees for a bow but is prevented by the IMPERIAL CENSOR who puts a finger to his lips. The BAILIFF nods to acknowledge his understanding)*

INSPECTOR HONG leaves the stage LOWER RIGHT and returns with his colleagues, MA and CHAO. The lights come on as JUDGE DEE enters without his legal robes and he paces around his office. They are all in the LOWER RIGHT of the stage is lit as the Judge's chambers. Scene continues.)

JUDGE DEE: Inspector, please have the Innkeeper identify the dead men and see if someone can examine the bodies to determine the cause of death.

INSPECTOR HONG: Yes, Your Honor.

JUDGE DEE: You might as well also search the Inn thoroughly for any sign of the goods.

INSPECTOR HONG: Yes, sir.

JUDGE DEE: Ma and Chao can help you with the search. Talk to everyone in the inn to find out all you can about the guests. (*With hands on his hips,*) I'd like to know what the neighbors think.

(*He paces in a small circle.*) While you're at it, ask about the relationship between the Innkeeper and the Constable. Make sure to give these people time to remember and answer your questions more fully.

(*Facing the Inspector.*) Have I forgotten anything?

INSPECTOR HONG: Perhaps we should talk to all the members of the Constable's clique.

JUDGE DEE (*nods*): Make it so, Inspector. This is a small village; if the murderer is from here, we should find out quite easily. If he is not from here, we need to act fast so that he does not get away; he already has a day's head-start.

MA: He won't travel as fast as we can if he is pushing two cartloads of silk.

JUDGE DEE (*looks at MA*): Ah, smart mouse! You will go far. I am glad you're on our side of the law. (*Smiles.*) All right then, let's meet here again first thing tomorrow morning and be ready to travel if the case is not closed. Inspector Hong, may I please have a word with you?

(*Ma and Chao exit; the Judge addresses the Inspector.*)

Did you notice the stranger in the courtroom?

INSPECTOR HONG: Yes sir. The Bailiff seemed to have had an exchange with him.

JUDGE DEE: Yes, he looked like a high official in disguise. I don't want to put the Bailiff in a tight spot, but ...

INSPECTOR HONG (*tactfully interrupting the Judge*): No sir. I could talk to him, but it might put him in an awkward position—you know his loyalty to you, but he seems to have made some sort of a promise to the stranger in disguise. We don't want to force the issue with him. But I don't think there is anything for you to worry about, Your Honor. The Imperial Court is probably just checking up on you and the stranger is a Censor. After all, your grandfather hired my father to work in your family and he was a Minister at the Imperial Court. Your father was a Prefect, almost a Governor. You sir, have no doubt attracted the Court's attention for the way you handled cases in your previous position in that small village.

JUDGE DEE: I suppose you are right (*clears his throat*) but I don't like being spied upon. I understand, however, it is necessary when

8

ruling this great empire. Great authority and latitude are given to Imperial officials and we cannot allow such officials to abuse their authority.

INSPECTOR HONG: If I may add, Your Honor…

JUDGE DEE: Of course.

INSPECTOR HONG: There is probably some concern over the assistants you hired to work with you as investigators.

JUDGE DEE (*with concern*): Do you suspect them of continuing in their old ways?

INSPECTOR HONG: Not at all, Your Honor. I am proud to serve with them. (*Beat.*) But the villagers have expressed uneasiness that you chose two former bandits and a former cat burglar, a woman even, as your investigators.

JUDGE DEE (*sighs*): I understand such worries, I think. But you must admit, I have chosen well. These three have initiative and courage. (*Thinks.*) I believe they deserve a second chance; what do you think?

INSPECTOR HONG: I believe that Your Honor's choices are inspired—very wise, perhaps even ingenious. (*He adds carefully and tactfully*): But honestly sir, if something were to go wrong, the fact that you chose these three would be held against you. Whether or not that is relevant, you are taking a gamble.

JUDGE DEE (*nodding*): As always, Inspector, you give good advice. We must be extra careful. But in the past few months, the three have proved invaluable.

INSPECTOR HONG (*with mock seriousness*): Some people might have complained, because you so rarely use the instruments of torture, that you are soft on crime.

JUDGE DEE (*with a cold smile*): Ha! That'll be the day.

(*Lights fade to black. Four beats. Lights come up again.*)

SCENE 2

(The next morning at the Judge's Chambers. This is set at LOWER RIGHT of the stage. Inspector Hong, Chao, and Ma are seated when the Judge enters.)

JUDGE DEE: Good morning, gentlemen. What do we know today that we did not yesterday? *(He sits.)*

MA: Innkeeper Gong is truly a miser. All his servants said so... I got the feeling that even his wife thinks so. Anyway, the inn attracts locals with food and drink while they play cards and dice and my parents made me promise to stay away from any of these places.

JUDGE DEE: Does that mean that Gong killed his guests? *(The others shrug.)*

INSPECTOR HONG: He identified one of the bodies the Constable found as Lu, one of the silk merchants at the inn. He says the other body is not that of the other guest, Shao. *(He stands.)* According to him, Shao is younger, taller, more muscular, and has a black front tooth. The second dead man is about fifty and looks familiar but I can't place him. He might be a farmer from outside the village.

JUDGE DEE *(perks up)*: If it's a local person, we should have a missing person report soon. Check with the nearest surrounding villages. *(Sneers.)* The constables there may be as efficient as the one we have here.

CHAO: I'll follow up on that.

JUDGE DEE: If the second body is someone from outside the area, we might have a new wrinkle in the investigation.

(As the JUDGE paces back and forth, the conference is interrupted by the BAILIFF, entering from LOWER LEFT.)

BAILIFF: Excuse me for intruding, Your Honor, but Mrs. Wang just reported her husband missing. She and her husband own the farm with the fish pond outside the village. He left home early two days ago but did not return as expected.

JUDGE DEE: Please take her to the dead bodies and see if she can identify either of them.

BAILIFF: Yes, Your Honor. *(He leaves LOWER LEFT.)*

MA: Some people in the village spoke of a group of leather merchants traveling through yesterday afternoon. The merchants said they had been at a rest stop when a tall man with a black tooth passed them from the opposite direction. They hailed him but he shouted back that he was in a hurry to get to the city. *(Looks around.)* He would have to pass through Turnip Town.

JUDGE DEE: Was he traveling fast?

MA: I heard that the leather merchants said the tall man was strong but was pushing a cart that looked overloaded and heavy ... that he was straining.

INSPECTOR HONG *(Stands up to address the Judge.)*: If he gets much beyond that little hamlet past Turnip Town, Garlic Gardens is the name I believe, he will be outside your jurisdiction.

JUDGE DEE *(thoughtfully)*: Inspector, would you please go to his Honor Magistrate Deng of the county and city beyond Garlic Gardens. Give him my compliments and tell him we request his assistance to arrest a murder suspect named Shao who is possibly traveling toward the city with the stolen silks. Provide him with the Innkeeper's description of Shao and ask if he would be so kind as to send two or three men to intercept him on each of the roads that lead from his village to ours.

INSPECTOR HONG: Do you think he will help us?

JUDGE DEE: He should—he gets credit for helping to solve a case of a double homicide. We will still have to do all the investigating until we find the culprit, the evidence, and get a confession out of him. I'd like you to get to Garlic Gardens before Shao does. See if you can borrow a fast horse from the stables in our village. If you see Shao, don't try to take him on yourself ... He has already killed two men.

(*As the INSPECTOR leaves LOWER RIGHT, JUDGE DEE turns to Ma and Chao.*) Ma, help Chao with checking the nearby villages, then go to Turnip Town to find out if the people there have seen anyone resembling Shao. I will leave early tomorrow to meet you there... (*shakes his head*) Garlic Gardens. (*Sighs.*) Turnip Town!

(*JUDGE DEE leaves LOWER RIGHT. Ma and Chao relax in their chairs.*)

CHAO: I say, I really like working with the Judge, don't you?

MA: Yes, the past couple of years have been interesting. We were looking for adventure when we left our villages and joined up with those bandits. I can't believe we actually tried to rob His Honor and the convoy bringing him here!

CHAO: Yeah! We were idiots then and very lucky to have met the judge so early in our days of sowing wild oats.

MA: Ha! Remember when he took off his robes and challenged us to a fight? Even though there were four of us! He must have serious gongfu training. I was sore for a week from one of his flying kicks. (*Rises to stretch.*)

CHAO: Our two companions had swords but with his walking stick the magistrate knocked their blades out of their hands.

MA: Yes, then the soldiers came. It must have been obvious to them we were a gang of bandits—I thought for sure the Judge would turn us in.

INSPECTOR HONG (*enters from LOWER RIGHT*): Don't let me interrupt.

MA: We're just chatting about the day we met you and the judge.

CHAO: Yes, the soldiers arrived and were all set to arrest us when the Judge told them that *he* had stopped us on our way and asked us to help him exercise! You remember?

INSPECTOR HONG: Of course. The judge said later that it was just intuition that prompted him to do so. (*He looks at each of them as if inspecting their clothes.*) I just came back to remind you that you fellows owe him your best behavior.

CHAO: No problem. I was convinced instantly that we should join him. Our two companions were real bandits and took off. I don't regret joining the Judge one bit.

MA: Neither do I. Life is still as exciting, and it's all legal!

INSPECTOR HONG: Remind me to tell Tao.

CHAO: Where is she anyway?

MA: Didn't she go visit her grandmother or something?

INSPECTOR HONG: Yes, her parents had sold her to be a servant in a rich household. She ran away and her grandmother took her in.

CHAO: Ah, so that's why she never talks about her parents ...

(All exit LOWER RIGHT. Lights fade quickly out then come up after four beats.)

SCENE 3

(Outside Turnip Town, the next day. JUDGE DEE, disguised as an herbalist, enters LOWER LEFT. He approaches an older man sitting at CENTER STAGE and rubbing his right shoulder.)

JUDGE DEE: Good afternoon, older brother. Looks to me like you've already done a full day's work.

OLD MAN (*grumpily*): When there's a grave to be dug, there's a grave to be dug, you know. No arguing about the when or why. I leave all that to the priests and the family.

JUDGE DEE: Oh, who died?

OLD MAN: The most important man in town, the butcher!

JUDGE DEE: Ah yes, where would we be if we did not get some pork or chicken from time to time! How did he die?

OLD MAN: They say he and his apprentice were getting some chickens ready for a banquet and one of the hens escaped. The butcher stepped quickly after it but slipped and fell on his own knife. Ai-yah! His wife had just come out with their lunch and saw the whole event. How she wailed!

JUDGE DEE: Did she accuse anyone? … Like the apprentice?

OLD MAN: No, I don't think so, no.

JUDGE DEE: I suppose the constable took their stories and agreed with them.

OLD MAN: Oh yes...You ask questions like the constable.

JUDGE DEE: Hm. It looks as if you have a pain in your shoulder.

OLD MAN (*grumpily*): Very observant of you. It's an old injury, but digging graves doesn't help, you know.

JUDGE DEE: If you will allow me to put a little pressure on one or two points and prescribe some herbs…

OLD MAN (*afraid of a scam*): I won't be able to pay you!

JUDGE DEE: Don't worry about that. (*Looks around.*) If there are some woods on a hill nearby, you can find this herb. (*He pats his pouch.*) Then it will all be free. As for what I give you, I'll consider it my good deed for the day … Maybe for the week.

(*JUDGE DEE takes out a small packet from his pouch and opens it before the old man. He picks out a sample and shows the old man*): See this combination of leaf and flower? It comes from bushes about as high as a man. Pluck the leaf and the flowers together and dry them for two weeks. They will keep for a year after that. Whenever you need relief from your pain, boil some, like making tea. Only remember to boil this herb for twice as long as tea leaves. You can have this package here, no charge. Now let me put some pressure on a couple of points on your shoulder.

(*As JUDGE DEE touches the OLD MAN, he immediately yells out*): Ah-ow!

JUDGE DEE (*firmly*): Brother, I haven't started yet! …Just take a deep breath and let it out slowly as I press, O.K.? I'll press for a count of ten. Then we wait the same amount of time and I'll do it again on a slightly different spot.

OLD MAN: You sure you know what you're doing?

(*JUDGE DEE begins his manipulation of the OLD MAN's shoulder while the conversation continues. As the Judge applies pressure on the old man's shoulder, he nods to keep time.*)

JUDGE DEE: Of course, even though I am not charging you anything. (*Trying to break the ice.*) So, have you seen any ghosts lately, eh?

OLD MAN (*Shudders and makes an unhappy face*): Not my favorite subject of conversation, you know?

JUDGE DEE (*nods and continues to keep time.*): Of course, I understand. How about living people? Any interesting individuals or groups come by lately? Horse traders, wood-cutters, silk merchants ...

OLD MAN (*after the first round of pressure on his shoulder, he moves his shoulder gingerly*): Nobody has come by the cemetery this whole year, except, you know ....

JUDGE DEE (*nods*): When the time comes, we must go. Sometimes we go with a large and noisy crowd, sometimes not so.

OLD MAN (*Remembering*): There was one last year that gave me a scare.

JUDGE DEE: A scare? (*Rubs his hands and begins second round of pressure on the old man's shoulder*)

OLD MAN: Ah, ah ... ah-h. (*He reacts to the pressure on his aching shoulder, inhales deeply and exhales slowly.*) Yes, it was an ordinary looking affair with the usual family, priests and monks, you know? But we had a difficult time with the coffin.

JUDGE DEE: A difficult time?

OLD MAN: Yes, it appeared as if the coffin didn't want to go, you know?

JUDGE DEE: What do you mean ... didn't want to go? Did you feel something, hear anything?

OLD MAN (*thinking and knocking his head with the knuckles of his right hand*): There may have been a knock ... like a nail hitting on wood ... when we dropped the coffin ... but it was the fact that we dropped the coffin that had me going ... I've worked here for thirty years and I can count on the fingers of one hand the number of times we have dropped the coffin. Usually it is clear someone slipped or tripped ... That time it felt like somebody or something didn't want to go someplace, a resistance. It was weird.

JUDGE DEE *(ends the second round of pressure)*: But the burial proceeded?

OLD MAN: Eventually. We struggled for a quarter of an hour or so. The widow and her daughter cried and wailed...Ha, that widow, what a handsome looking woman, even in sackcloth and white.

JUDGE DEE: And that's the most exciting thing that has happened last year?

OLD MAN: Pretty much. (*He stands up and walks around a small circle, swinging his right arm.*)

JUDGE DEE: How's the shoulder?

OLD MAN: Good, thank you very much. I don't know how to repay you, you know?

JUDGE DEE: My good deed ... Are you sure you didn't see a silk merchant pushing a cart?

OLD MAN: I'm sure. The cemetery is a little off the main road, you know? Well, thanks again. I must be off now. Good day to you.

(OLD MAN exits STAGE LEFT while JUDGE DEE shakes out his shoulders and hands. He walks across to STAGE RIGHT and sits down. He looks around and sees an old woman, MOTHER BEE,

moving with difficulty as she enters from UPPER LEFT carrying several bundles and leading a young girl, heading LOWER LEFT.)

JUDGE DEE *(stands up)*: Ah auntie, may I help you?

MOTHER BEE: Oh, thank you, but I don't want to take you out of your way. I live outside the village (*nods off LOWER LEFT*).

JUDGE DEE: Please let me carry your bundles at least to the village gate. Do you live far from there?

(They start walking towards LOWER LEFT.)

MOTHER BEE: No, it is a short distance from the village gate to my son's residence. He died last year so it's just us and my daughter-in-law. She is a very proper and chaste widow and never leaves the house. (*She stops.*) In fact, she won't allow visitors either.

JUDGE DEE: I see. So, she insists on maintaining her proper station as a widow. (*Rearranges the bundles he is carrying.*) But what she is doing is very strict! She and her husband must have been very religious.

MOTHER BEE *(conveying a happy secret)*: I don't know about that, but there were a lot of dinner parties while he was alive.

JUDGE DEE: And is this lovely little girl ... your grand-daughter?

(Little girl tries to respond but gags.)

MOTHER BEE *(sadly)*: Yes, unfortunately she is unable to speak.

JUDGE DEE: Oh dear, was she born that way? How old is she?

MOTHER BEE: She is nearly six and was as talkative as could be until recently ... First my son fell ill and died, and then she fell ill and lost her voice. We thought it was temporary but it seems to be quite permanent. She is very intelligent and obedient though and helps where she can in the house.

JUDGE DEE: Ah, good girl.

(JUDGE DEE pats the girl on her shoulder. He continues):

It must have been a terrible epidemic to have killed your son and struck your granddaughter dumb. When did these misfortunes happen?

MOTHER BEE: About a year ago, during the Dragon Boat Festival. My son became ill that night—upset stomach, vomiting. He was dead by the morning. My granddaughter caught a cold and became mute three or four days after that. *(Sighs.)* I suppose we are born to suffer ... Here we are, the village gate. Thank you for all your kindness.

JUDGE DEE: Not at all. Tell me where you live; I have some skill with herbs and will bring some in a few days and let's see if we can't cure your granddaughter.

MOTHER BEE *(gesturing off stage):* Ah, we live over there near a stream. You will see it if you turn left after passing through that gate. But please don't bother to come. As I said, my daughter-in-law does not permit visitors to our house.

(Widow struggles with her bundles. The Judge watches her struggle with her bundles for a beat and decides.)

JUDGE DEE: At least let me carry these bundles until you can see your house. I really hope we meet again soon and you will let me treat your granddaughter. I know just the herbs that will cure her (*with emphasis*) provided she was not born mute.

MOTHER BEE *(with conviction):* I assure you she used to chatter like the sparrows and sing like the orioles.

JUDGE DEE: Then I guarantee that she will talk again.

(They all exit, LOWER LEFT. JUDGE DEE quickly re-enters and walks back into CENTER STAGE where he meets Ma and Chao who enter from REAR STAGE LEFT.)

JUDGE DEE: Hello, friends! Have you had an eventful journey?

MA: On the way from Six Mile Village we met some farmers who had run into a silk merchant pushing a cart that seemed to be very heavy. They said that they had asked him about his goods and he got angry so there was a fight. (*Leans in conversationally.*) They might actually have been trying to steal from Shao but apparently, he is very strong. (*Ma and Chao pantomime a fight scene.*) He kicked one of them and punched another before they all gave up. They described him as a tall young man with a black front tooth.

CHAO: Whether or not the farmers were trying to get some silk, they clearly got the worse of it—I saw one of them limping heavily and another rubbing his left arm as if it was still sore. That Shao certainly appears to be a strong and violent man. I wouldn't want to run into him by myself.

JUDGE DEE (*Thinks, nods, then speaks slowly*): The two of you should move on to Garlic Garden and Lame Ox Village.

CHAO: (*Nodding.*) We can do that, but we'll have to separate. Those villages are on two different roads to the city.

JUDGE DEE: Yes, with luck Judge Deng's men will have intercepted the murderer whichever road he took. If not, use your discretion and whoever catches up with Shao should keep him in sight until the soldiers from Judge Deng show up. You may have to spend the night in the city and bring Shao back the next day. Inspector Hong will meet you there to help bring Shao back to our village.

MA: How do you want us to handle the questions?

22

JUDGE DEE: Judge Deng will have authority unless he hands Shao to you. In that case, give Shao no food or water but do not begin the interrogation until we get him back to Six Mile Village. I shall be back there tomorrow. I want to snoop around here for the rest of today. Meet me in my chambers before noon tomorrow.

CHAO (*speaking as they turn to leave*): Your Honor.

JUDGE DEE: Yes?

CHAO: Ma and I want to say we really enjoy working with you. We are grateful you didn't hold the little bit of banditry against us.

JUDGE DEE (*nodding*): I thought you were sowing your wild oats in the marshes and needed to get something out of your fantasies. Heroes of the Three Kingdoms did that ... But some of the people in the village are nervous about having the likes of you two and Tao around.

MA: Have no fear, Your Honor. We are not going back to our old ways. The villagers might be nervous, but they should get used to us.

JUDGE DEE (*shrugs and lifts his hands*): These villagers have not seen change in many, many generations.

(*Lights fade to black. They come up after four beats to the next scene.*)

SCENE 4

(Turnip Town, same day. This scene is at a bath-house with natural hot springs located onstage at LOWER LEFT. Chen, a childhood friend of BEE, is soaking in the pool when the Judge enters. He is still disguised as an herbalist.)

JUDGE DEE: Excuse me if you were expecting to enjoy some quiet time with your own thoughts.

CHEN: No problem, you are welcome, friend. (*Waves a hand.*) My family name is Chen, a common name, but our own. This spring is about the only thing our village can be proud of ... other than our turnips of course *(laughs cheerily)*.

JUDGE DEE: My family name is Dee. Do many visitors come here?

CHEN: Not really. (*Gestures around.*) It is not a big spring and there have been no stories of miracles performed here.

JUDGE DEE: A quiet spring in a quiet village. And the water is nice and hot. A-ah! *(JUDGE DEE slips into the pool. He and CHEN face each other, perhaps in a vee-shaped arrangement with the point towards the audience.)* You get the occasional traveling salesman?

CHEN: Once in a while someone stays long enough, but usually they just pass through. Times are hard.

JUDGE DEE: I hear that silk and leather merchants have been passing through lately.

CHEN: Is that so? Are you looking for a particular person?

JUDGE DEE: Yes. I am only a traveling herbalist, but in the city someone did me a kindness once and told me that if I wanted to

24

repay him, to pass on the blessing as it were, to look for a young, tall silk merchant named Shao and treat him to a meal.

CHEN (*shakes his head slowly*): Sorry, I can't help you there.

JUDGE DEE: That's all right ... Do you usually come here by yourself?

CHEN: Lately yes, but until a year ago, I often came with my school-mate. He was a fisherman named Bee in the village with a very successful business. He worked hard and kept the village well supplied with fish and oysters.

JUDGE DEE: What happened?

CHEN: He died last year. It was quite mysterious.

JUDGE DEE (*with mild curiosity*): Mysterious?

CHEN: Yes. Sudden ... One night he and his beautiful wife entertained me to dinner—it was at the Dragon Boat Festival, the fifth day of the fifth month last year. They lived in a nice house by the stream outside this village. The next day he was dead.

JUDGE DEE: Did they fight or quarrel?

CHEN: I don't *think* so. (*Shrugs.*) I know his wife was trying to get him to move into a bigger house. His mother told me that he had a bad night after the dinner—stomach pains, vomiting and so forth. Then ...

JUDGE DEE: That's too bad. What did the magistrate say?

CHEN: Oh, there was nothing to report or complain about. His mother, that is Mother Bee, and his widow, Widow Bee, told the constable all about it and everyone agreed that it was some illness. His daughter got it too, except that she did not die, she just became mute.

JUDGE DEE: (*Realizes with a start that he had talked to the woman's mother earlier in the day.*) Really? Sounds like quite an epidemic in the village.

CHEN (*pauses for a beat to think*): No, I don't recall that anyone else in the village was sick at that time. The funeral was odd though; the grave-diggers claimed to be having difficulty getting the coffin into the ground (*He sits up.*) Maybe they were trying to get a bigger tip. Ha! (*Swishes water around.*) But Widow Bee seems to have changed her life completely. Before her husband's death she was always eager to go out, to see and be seen, as they say. After the funeral, she has become the model of a chaste widow, she does not go out at all and receives no visitors ... That's a real shame; she was always a sight for sore eyes.

(*CHEN gets up to leave.*)

JUDGE DEE: Had enough?

CHEN: Yes ... I don't want my parents to think I am indifferent to their welfare. (*Makes a wry face and sighs.*) It is difficult to meet all the expectations of the old dears. I should get back to the farm, even though there is nothing to do there today.

(*JUDGE DEE waves Chen off the stage UPPER LEFT. Then he gets up as Inspector Hong enters through that exit.*)

JUDGE DEE: Inspector, I was about to leave.

INSPECTOR HONG: We could walk back to the Village as if we just met here.

JUDGE DEE: Good, we can talk about some matters that have made me curious.

(*The Inspector checks the exit and nods to signal all clear.*)

JUDGE DEE: First I met an old man, a grave digger, who told of what he called "a strange burial" a year ago. It seems a coffin resisted going into the ground.

(*He looks at the Inspector as if questioning him. The Inspector shrugs.*) Then I helped an old woman with her bags. It appears her son, a fisherman named Bee, died a year ago. The woman, Mother Bee, lived with him, his wife, and a granddaughter.

INSPECTOR HONG: So, the Widow and the Mother can comfort each other, how traditional and cozy.

JUDGE DEE: Yes. Then my companion here at the springs just told me Bee was his best friend …

INSPECTOR HONG (*in a noncommittal tone*): People say, when you have a hammer, you see a lot of nails.

JUDGE DEE (*stands straight as if at "Attention"*): My grandfather was a minister in the imperial court. My father was a provincial governor. And I was taught to burn incense every morning and evening in reverence for their memory.

(*They leave. The lights fade to black for four beats, and then come up again for the next scene.*)

SCENE 5

(The next day, back in Judge Dee's chambers at Six Mile Village. Inspector Hong, Ma, and Chao enter, followed by Judge Dee.)

INSPECTOR HONG: Welcome back, Your Honor.

JUDGE DEE: Thank you. Do we have Shao?

MA: We certainly do. He is in the holding cell and he says he is thirsty.

JUDGE DEE: Has he confessed to the murders?

CHAO: Not yet.

JUDGE DEE *(Slowly nodding)*: Let's keep him without food or water for another day.

(Turning to the investigators) Ma and Chao, question him again about the silk that he had—where he had bought the silk, that sort of thing. You should check with the usual vendors. Then take him to his cell and put him in the smelliest one that we have. On the way to it, make sure he gets a good look at the torture chamber. *(Emphasis on "torture chamber.")* Explain to him that under our legal system, when a capital crime has been committed, we *must* get a confession.

MA *(melodramatically)*: The jailer is really disappointed that he has had so little use of his instruments of torture since you became magistrate.

JUDGE DEE *(chuckles)*: Really? Tell him to explain to Shao the various instruments and how he looks forward to using them ... I believe that if we can get Shao to admit to his crime without actually torturing him, no one should care.

CHAO: No one is as humane as Your Honor, but we were only joking about our jailer. He is not one who enjoys inflicting pain.

JUDGE DEE: It has its place ... but I find that a day or two without food or water or access to toilet facilities usually works. If a suspect appears to be particularly stubborn, then the (*exaggerated stage whisper*) *water torture treatment* should be enough. In any case, it is bad karma to inflict pain and suffering.

MA: Well, we have strong evidence against Shao. The Innkeeper can identify him and I doubt that he can explain how his companion Lu died or how he came to have twice as much silk as a merchant normally carts around.

CHAO: Further, we have told him that he has been identified in a fight with some farmers near Turnip Town. He admitted to being ill-tempered on that particular day and gave us a long incoherent story.

(*Hesitates and looks at Inspector Hong, who nods, but still addressing the Judge*) Does Your Honor wish to add to what we know about the homicides?

JUDGE DEE: No. I didn't learn anything new about this case on my visit to Turnip Town, but I did learn about another possible capital crime.

MA: We haven't completely wrapped up this double homicide investigation yet!

CHAO (*nudges MA*): What can we do to help?

JUDGE DEE: Here's the story, tell me what you think. About a year ago—

MA: A year ago?

JUDGE DEE (*nods impatiently*): —a man had dinner with his family and friends. Then he has a bad night, maybe from something he ate or a cold he caught. (*Paces in a small circle*) He suffers stomach pains, vomiting, that sort of thing. The next day his family finds him dead. There is no police report written because both his widow and his mother are convinced, so they said, that this was a matter of illness, natural causes. (*He crouches and speaks with intensity.*) A few days later, his daughter caught a cold and lost her voice. Does this sound like fate or a random sequence of events? (*Paces around again.*) I actually met his little girl and her grandmother quite by accident. The old lady was walking home with her baskets.

CHAO: Why was the old lady doing the shopping instead of her daughter-in-law?

JUDGE DEE: That's what I thought! When I offered to visit with some herbs that would restore the child's voice, the grandmother said that's impossible. Because her daughter-in-law has become a chaste widow and never leaves the house *and* does not allow any visitors.

MA: Was there an epidemic at the village at that time?

JUDGE DEE: Not according to the mother or the dead man's classmate and good friend, a mister Chen. I met him in the bathhouse; it was a purely coincidental meeting.

MA (*facetiously*): We noticed the hot springs and fought the temptation to visit it.

JUDGE DEE (*in a long-suffering tone*): He told me that he and his friend, a fisherman named Bee, visited it often. The old woman I met earlier pointed out where their house is. It turns out she is

Mother Bee, the dead man's mother. The dead man's wife, Widow Bee, and her child live with her mother-in-law. I think Chao should go and observe the house for a week. (*Looks around.*) Tao is back from visiting her grandmother, isn't she? Take her with you and have her talk to the neighbors. Find out what anyone has to say about the fisherman and his family.

CHAO: Neighbors always talk. I mean, it helps to pass the time in the villages (*shrugs*). If the good widow has received any visitors, someone must have seen it and will talk about it.

MA (*waving his hands like a cat scratching*): Tao used to be a very good, er, burglar before Your Honor recruited her ...

JUDGE DEE (*shakes his head*): I don't think she will need those skills, at least not yet. I just want surveillance on the house for a week and a quiet visit to all the neighbors within a mile. People tend to talk more openly with a woman, I've noticed. One of you might also visit the cemetery and talk to the priests at the temple near it.

MA (*jokingly*): Yes, if there have been any wandering ghosts, I'm sure they'll be happy to talk about them.

JUDGE DEE (*with a straight face*): You never know.

(*Lights fade to black. Four beats. Lights come up for next scene.*)

SCENE 6

(*A few hours later, in a jail cell LOWER RIGHT. INSPECTOR HONG interrogates SHAO—both are seated—while a CLERK sits at a small table in the background. CHAO and MA lounge just outside the jail cell.*)

INSPECTOR HONG (*waving the air in front of his face and wrinkling his nose*): So, how did you and the other silk merchant meet.

SHAO (*hesitantly*): We ... met at the silk market out west.

INSPECTOR HONG: Were you friends?

SHAO: We ... became ...better acquainted on the road.

INSPECTOR HONG: What happened the day you left Six Mile Village?

SHAO: My companion and I pushed our carts across the village. We met someone who claimed Lu owed him some money. Lu said the argument was likely to take a while and urged me to take his silk and continue.

INSPECTOR HONG: Were they arguing?

SHAO: Yes. It looked like they might even start fighting. They shouted at each other.

INSPECTOR HONG: So, Lu gave you his silk?

SHAO (*nods*): To take to the market. We were going to meet in the next town and share the proceeds.

INSPECTOR HONG: Did he give you the receipts from his purchases of the silk?

SHAO: Ye-es... But I can't find them. I may have dropped them when the farmers attacked me. They were trying to steal the silk, you know.

INSPECTOR HONG (*shakes his head*): Are you sure, Old Shao? Maybe you never had the receipts. Maybe we found them on Lu's body. (*He gets up and walks slowly around Shao.*) Maybe we have examined his body and his clothes? And we have even discovered that someone has gone through them, looking for the receipts? Did you know he had a purse tied to his neck? Did you look there ... hm?

SHAO: I ... I.

INSPECTOR HONG (*Stands straight as if at "attention" and shakes his head gravely*): There were no signs of a fight where the two bodies were found. No one who lives in that area remembers hearing any arguments that morning. Our examination of the bodies showed that each man had been killed by a blow to the neck by someone very strong.

(*SHAO's defiant posture slumps, the Inspector continues*): What really happened, Shao?

(*SHAO remains sullenly silent.*)

INSPECTOR HONG: You don't really want to be tortured, do you? (*He sits.*) The evidence is very clear. Two men check into an inn, you and Lu. He is found dead the next day. Beside him is the body of a farmer from outside the village. Meanwhile, you have been caught with twice as much silk as a merchant normally carries. Several witnesses have identified you with an overloaded cart at various stages of your journey from Six Mile Village—a young, tall and strong man with a black tooth ...

SHAO (*shakily*): How did you find me so quickly?

INSPECTOR HONG (*nodding*): The bodies you left would have been found that day but no one would have known that the dead men, at least one of them, had been guests at the inn. Unfortunately for you, our constable has a grudge against the innkeeper.

SHAO: So, he filed a complaint? (*Shouts.*) This is so unfair! (*Wails.*) So unfair!

INSPECTOR HONG: You have no right to speak of anything as unfair. You have killed two men…

SHAO (*with his head down, he shakes his head for three beats*): I did it for her.

INSPECTOR HONG: Hm.

SHAO: Could I please have some water? (*Hong waves at those beyond the jail bars and someone brings a large jug and a cup.*) She said she would marry me if I had my own silk store and did not have to travel all around the countryside to buy and sell silk.

INSPECTOR HONG (*stands and paces slowly*): There is a big difference between traveling from village to village and those who sit in town minding their own stores.

SHAO (*nodding*): That's what she wanted, a life of comfort and status…And I wanted her.

INSPECTOR HONG: You cannot please women sometimes …

SHAO (*sniffs*): I am sure she wasn't just looking for a soft life.

INSPECTOR HONG: Did you know her family?

SHAO (*nodding*): I knew the family before they moved from our old village. She told me she had observed her cousins and friends and concluded life with a traveling salesman was too uncertain. She didn't need luxury, but wanted a stable family life.

INSPECTOR HONG (*calmly but firmly*): How many more men would you have to kill?

SHAO: Perhaps that is a life beyond our reach. (*Sobs.*) But I was not thinking. When Lu and I met that farmer, it seemed too good an opportunity …

INSPECTOR HONG (*looks closely at Shao in silence, then he stands by his seat and says*): The clerk will write up your confession. You will sign it. The penalty for murder is death, but at least you will be in a clean cell and comfortable until the sentence is approved. As you know, all executions must be approved by the Imperial authorities.

(*All exit when lights fade for four beats and then come up on the JUDGE in his chambers with INSPECTOR HONG.*)

JUDGE DEE: Woman trouble, somehow it doesn't seem to be in Shao's character—to have been so infatuated. He seemed stronger, more self-centered. (*Shakes his head.*) Men do strange things when there is a woman I suppose. It is certainly not the woman's fault that he chose to kill two men.

INSPECTOR HONG: There are greedy women and greedy men.

JUDGE DEE: Yes, yes, of course. That is why we have to investigate to determine who is guilty!

INSPECTOR HONG: Where do you think the other case, of the "reluctant corpse," will lead?

JUDGE DEE: Well, it is not as if the killer will escape if we don't find him … the victim died a year ago! On the other hand, I find the circumstances intriguing, even suspicious.

INSPECTOR HONG: Let's see now. A man dies and his wife becomes a strictly chaste widow.

JUDGE DEE (*animatedly*): There is something there that does not ring true, Inspector. I respect the values of our ancestors, but a woman with such concern for traditional proprieties. I think her first concern would be to support the mother of her dead spouse.

INSPECTOR HONG: Ah, you suspect Widow Bee of deception in acting the chaste widow, while neglecting her mother-in-law.

JUDGE DEE (*shaking his head*): You should have been there to see Mother Bee huffing and puffing with her packages and the poor little granddaughter trying to help. I am very curious to hear what Chao and Tao discover. Both Chen and Mother Bee said that the couple had been fond of merry-making and enjoying the company of others. (*Sternly*.) If there is even a whiff of evidence that the chaste widow act is mere pretense, there will be an investigation of the widow!

INSPECTOR HONG: I agree, Your Honor, but we must proceed cautiously. If the Widow did commit this murder, she has proven herself to be strong-willed and devious. She will probably give us a hard time with our investigations.

JUDGE DEE: Ah yes, she might even claim to be a woman being taken advantage of (*he sniffs*), harassment and so forth. (*As if struck by a new thought*) Also, I wonder how the daughter became mute.

INSPECTOR HONG (*shocked*): Oh dear, did the Widow kill her husband and then drug her own daughter?

JUDGE DEE (*with sympathy but firmly*): You are not getting queasy about investigations of this sort, I hope.

INSPECTOR HONG: Good heavens, no. But the girl ... reminds me of my daughter at that age.

JUDGE DEE (*gradually gets worked up*): I'm trying to keep an open mind about this, but the evidence suggests a murder. Then the use of herbs to cause the little girl to become mute and above all the hypocrisy of pretending to be the chaste widow—it is a travesty of a social and cultural ideal!

(*Lights fade to black. End of Act I, INTERMISSION.*)

ACT 2, SCENE 1

(*Two days later, the act and scene opens with the Courtroom of JUDGE DEE. On stage are the BAILIFF, INNKEEPER GONG and WIDOW LEE. The IMPERIAL CENSOR in disguise sits in the shadows. Two clerks sit at a table in front of JUDGE DEE's chair to transcribe the proceedings.*)

BAILIFF: The Court of the Honorable Judge Dee is now in session. All rise!

(*JUDGE DEE enters and sits, signaling with a wave that all present may also sit.*)

JUDGE DEE: Innkeeper Gong, I understand you have a complaint.

INNKEEPER GONG (*rises to speak*): Yes, Your Honor. I accuse Widow Lee of fraud. She came to my inn two days ago and … has eaten well. When I asked her today how long she intended to stay and when she would pay, she told me flat out that she had no money and offered to work for what she owed. (*Clears his throat*) I have since determined that her daughter was married into the family of the gentry Hua in the next village. The daughter unfortunately died on her wedding night last month, but the Hua family has been generous in letting the Widow Lee stay there.

JUDGE DEE (*with cold contempt*): And you think that the Hua family should pay for the Widow's stay at your inn?

INNKEEPER GONG (*earnestly*): Your Honor, I think someone should. (*He sits.*)

JUDGE DEE: I see. Widow Lee, what do you say?

WIDOW LEE (*stands and speaks with dignity*): What the Innkeeper says is true. My daughter, my only child, was betrothed to the oldest son of the Retired Prefect Hua. The family agreed that I could move in to live with them. (*She pauses to control a sob.*) When my daughter died, Young Hua, her husband of only one day, told me that I should stay. After a few weeks there, however, I have concluded that this is not a suitable arrangement.

JUDGE DEE (*tactfully*): The Hua family is well known for its generosity and traditional values.

WIDOW LEE: Yes, Your Honor. But the young man has a bright future. Last year, a few months before the wedding, he passed the Imperial exams with high honors. Someday soon he will remarry … he *must* remarry … to fulfill his obligation to continue his family line, if nothing else.

JUDGE DEE (*nods and speaks dreamily*): It is inevitable that he will feel the generations of his ancestors calling on him to do his part to perpetuate the family name.

WIDOW LEE (*nods*): That's what I mean. Then he might even be sent to serve the Imperial Court in another province… (*She stifles a sob.*) My presence would be an inconvenience to the family, an embarrassment.

JUDGE DEE (*with sympathy*): Why did you stay at the Gong inn?

WIDOW LEE (*gathers herself*): I heard that the inn is looking for workers so I applied for a position. But when I arrived … my nerves failed me ... I was so tired and hungry, it felt easier to order a meal and take a room to rest.

JUDGE DEE: What can you do for an inn?

INNKEEPER GONG (*rising*): But…

JUDGE DEE (*addressing the Innkeeper firmly*): Isn't it true that you are looking for workers?

INNKEEPER GONG (*as if seeking an eye for an eye, gesturing wildly*): But this woman defrauded me. She should be punished!

JUDGE DEE (*drily*): Innkeeper, I think I am supposed to determine whether and how she should be punished.

INNKEEPER GONG (*hangs his head*): Yes, Your Honor. (*He sits.*)

JUDGE DEE: Widow Lee?

WIDOW LEE (*Calmly answers the previous question*): I can sew, cook, clean house, and whatever I do not know how to do, I can learn.

JUDGE DEE (*tactfully*): You must realize that the Hua family may be embarrassed by the fact that some people might think they forced you to do this.

WIDOW LEE: I understand and will do everything I can to let it be known that I am doing this of my own free will. (*Blows her nose.*) When I left the Hua household, I did leave a note to this effect … In a few months, after my nerves settle, I hope to visit the family and pay my respects to Elder Hua, the patriarch of the family, for his kindness and hospitality.

JUDGE DEE (*decisively*): Innkeeper, I propose that you employ Widow Lee. (*The Innkeeper slaps his forehead.*) Since she has eaten and stayed at your fine establishment for two days, you need not pay her for the first month. In my opinion, one month of free labor is sufficient compensation for two days' worth of room and board as a guest at the inn—do you object?

(*The Innkeeper agonizes visibly before nodding and accepting the Judge's proposal. The Judge continues*):

40

After this month, you will decide what you shall pay her. (*Addressing the Innkeeper firmly*) It must be a fair wage…During all this time, the first month and thereafter, you must treat her as one of your servants. I believe you provide them all with meals and a place to sleep … You are not to mistreat the Widow. Do you agree?

INNKEEPER GONG (*Reluctantly, he stands and says*): I agree, Your Honor.

JUDGE DEE: Court may adjourn, but I would like to ask Widow Lee to stay for a little while… I am interested to learn about the death of her daughter since it appears to have been unreported.

INNKEEPER GONG: Of course, Your Honor.

JUDGE DEE: Very well. (*Nods to BAILIFF.*)

BAILIFF: The Court of the Honorable Judge Dee is now adjourned. All rise!

(*As the Courtroom empties, lights fade to create a pool of light that serves as JUDGE DEE's office. JUDGE DEE, INSPECTOR HONG and WIDOW LEE step into the light.*)

JUDGE DEE: Widow Lee, would you please tell me what happened to cause your daughter's death?

WIDOW LEE: I don't know, but several people told me on that wedding night and during the reception, the couple had been teased, some say excessively, by another man, Young Hu. He is a classmate of Young Hua, the groom, and passed his exams at the same time. For a while he was also a suitor for my daughter's hand in marriage.

JUDGE DEE: Ah. But do you think the teasing had anything to do with your daughter's death?

WIDOW LEE (*without hesitation*): I do not. Nor do I think that Young Hu could in any way have caused my daughter's death. She died in a horrible, horrible fashion … The couple had just retired for the night when Young Hua ran out of the bedroom crying that his bride was seriously ill. She cried of stomach pains, and had spasms and convulsions for a couple of hours … I was there all the time … till her agony stopped and she died.

JUDGE DEE (*Shakes his head*): Why no police report?

WIDOW LEE: Elder Hua, the retired prefect, questioned all the guests and servants at the house that evening. He determined that no one had any motive or opportunity to kill my daughter and therefore the whole incident was an act of fate. Hence, no report.

JUDGE DEE (*Nods thoughtfully*): Young Hu—you said he could not have done it. Why did some speak of his excessive teasing?

WIDOW LEE (*firmly*): I don't remember now whether that was loose talk from the guests or servants. But I myself do not believe that young man is capable of killing my daughter.

JUDGE DEE: The Hu family is also of the gentry class, I believe.

WIDOW LEE: Yes … My daughter was very fortunate to have attracted the attention of such eligible young men.

JUDGE DEE (*shaking his head*): I don't see how teasing, excessive or not, could have led to spasms and convulsions—do you?

(*The JUDGE looks at both the WIDOW and the INSPECTOR. Both shake their heads.*)

JUDGE DEE (*Stands, summing up*): If you don't mind, Widow Lee, I shall call on the Hua family in the next few days. I know of Elder Hua by reputation. (*He shrugs.*) He will no doubt think I am impertinent to concern myself over an affair he has deemed closed.

I shall have to remind him somehow that although he was an esteemed Prefect, he is now retired, while I, though a lowly Magistrate, am still in service and responsible for the safety of that portion of the Empire entrusted into my care.

WIDOW LEE (*Stands and dips her head and shoulders towards the Judge*): I am only a poor widow and cannot presume to advise Your Honor in this matter.

(*Lights fade to black and the scene ends.*)

ACT 2, SCENE 2

(*JUDGE DEE's office, LOWER RIGHT, the following week. CHAO, TAO and INSPECTOR HONG are with the Judge who is seated.*)

JUDGE DEE: You have news about Widow Bee and the case of the reluctant corpse, I hope.

CHAO: We do, Your Honor. (*He glances at Tao who gestures for him to proceed.*) I maintained surveillance on the entrance of the house for a whole week and saw nobody visiting, only Mother Bee coming and going, sometimes accompanied by her granddaughter. But Tao—

(*CHAO makes a grand gesture to his colleague, TAO, and steps back.*)

TAO (*eagerly*): I talked to the neighbors the first three days, and everyone reported that there had been no visitors to the Bee family since the husband died. They were all quick to add that they found this strange as the family had been active socially, especially Widow Bee herself. Everyone agrees that she is a most attractive woman.

JUDGE DEE (*in a tone that conveys disapproval of gossip/hearsay*): What does everyone think of her character?

TAO: I did not ask, Your Honor. That is a delicate subject ...

JUDGE DEE (*reflects for a moment on TAO's hesitation to speak on questions of character*): No doubt. Did you see anything yourself?

TAO: Yes, Your Honor. After I was done questioning the neighbors, I went to watch the back of the house—the Widow's rooms are on that side of the building. The windows have heavy curtains but once, (*coughs*) only once, the curtains over one of the windows opened. A

44

man appeared for a moment before a woman's hand closed the curtains.

JUDGE DEE: You saw a man? Can you identify him?

CHAO (*with a look at Tao who looks at the ground*): Your Honor, Tao is too modest to say so but from her description—he was tall, fair, and very handsome—several of the neighbors recognized a man known as Young Su. He is the oldest son of Elder Su, a well-known local landlord ... Everyone says the son is quite handsome. He also has, er, something of a reputation of a fondness for the ladies.

JUDGE DEE (*Stands and paces slowly*): Ah, and how did that young man get into the house if the neighbors did not observe anything? ... Is the house adjacent to any other buildings? (*He glances at Chao and Tao who shrug, then says decisively.*) We must consult the property records for the area and look for adjoining buildings. Those records may contain information, even diagrams that could guide the investigation. Inspector Hong, please make sure this is done as soon as possible.

(*He pauses to think again. Then he continues*):

So, Chao, did you or Tao ask at the temple if the monks observed any ... irregularity ... at the funeral?

TAO (*with a slight swagger of worldliness or sophistication*): I did Your Honor, although I am not sure of the value of superstition in our investigation.

JUDGE DEE: It may be superstition to us, but what do the people there think? What did they say happened?

TAO: The monks remember that there was a fuss at the burial. At the cemetery, we spoke with an old grave-digger, a grumpy old man who confirmed this and said that he felt the coffin was "resisting" burial. The temple monks were informed about this then and discussed it with the family. They suggested that special prayers be said and sutras be recited at the temple.

JUDGE DEE: How did the family react to that?

TAO: They agreed after some … discussion … about how much would be spent. They also requested that the ceremonies be kept private.

JUDGE DEE: Is that unusual around here?

CHAO: No, Your Honor. But many families like to have large and loud ceremonies in which they and their neighbors participate. That way, they believe, the benefit of such prayers and rituals is spread over the whole neighborhood.

(*JUDGE DEE remains standing with his arms folded and chin in his right hand. His investigators wait courteously, making only small and unobtrusive gestures to each other to suggest their inability to follow the JUDGE's line of thought.*)

JUDGE DEE: I think we should exhume the body. (*The investigators gasp audibly.*) Nobody here is superstitious, I hope. (*The JUDGE looks around.*) The death is mysterious and the reasons given—an illness, something he ate—might make sense except for two things: that the daughter has become mute without good reason and that the widow's behavior defies common sense as well as traditional values.

TAO: Do we have the authority to do that, Your Honor?

JUDGE DEE: Yes, it is amazing how much authority I have to solve capital crimes. (*Stands and shakes his head.*) I am not sure that I approve of this, but I have the authority.

INSPECTOR HONG: You suspect her?

46

JUDGE DEE (*clearly but circumspectly*): I do not believe it is any sort of piety that has led her to maintain her strict seclusion.

TAO: We will check on the background of the family house and all adjacent property. That may yield something we can work on. Young Su's appearance may be a big deal, but we only saw him once.

CHAO (*accepts blame with chagrin*): My mistake for keeping the surveillance only on the front entrance.

JUDGE DEE: Well, let's find out how many entrances there are. The property records and diagrams should be straightforward on this. Someone should investigate Young Su and question him. At some point during the questioning you should ask him if he has visited the Widow ... Meanwhile we will proceed with the exhumation of the body, but I can wait two days for the results of a search of the property documents.

INSPECTOR HONG (*Suggests tactfully*): Do you want to visit Elder Hua about the strange death of his daughter-in-law before ... or after all this?

JUDGE DEE (*smiles to acknowledge the Inspector's tact*): Well, Inspector, what do you recommend?

INSPECTOR HONG: Your Honor, it is *possible* to visit Elder Hua tomorrow or the next day. We should send him notice at once that you will call on him to acquaint yourself with the facts about the unexpected death of his daughter-in-law—in your role as the guardian of public safety for this county.

(*JUDGE DEE paces and nods. INSPECTOR HONG continues*):

In the meantime, we will examine the documents related to the property occupied by the Bee family and its neighbor or neighbors.

The paperwork for the exhumation can also be prepared during this time.

JUDGE DEE: So, all this is *possible*, but what do you *recommend*?

INSPECTOR HONG: I believe we might need Your Honor's guidance while we examine the documents pertaining to the Bee case and also in the preparation of the order for the exhumation. We would then be able to visit Elder Hua a day or two later. He would appreciate the courtesy of the additional notice.

JUDGE DEE (*nods and smiles*): Very well, Inspector. I shall try not to rush things. You and I should compose the order for exhumation and the notice to Elder Hua. Chao, get Ma to join you in examining the documents relating to the Bee residence and the properties around it.

(*The Judge steps toward Tao and continues speaking*):

Tao, I would like you to deliver the notice to Elder Hua when it is ready. Find an excuse to stay and talk some more with the servants. Ask about the guests who were in the bride's company and ... question the servants who waited on the bridal couple. (*He cups his chin in his right hand and walks in a small circle slowly.*) I also want you to take a good look around the house. See how the rooms lead from one to another. I am particularly interested in where the bride was during the afternoon and evening of the wedding.

INSPECTOR HONG: Do you know something we should, Your Honor?

JUDGE DEE: It is only a hunch, Inspector. This death does not appear to be the result of malice nor can I imagine any motive for it. I think Elder Hua was right to refer to it as an act of fate. But if we can find out more about the circumstances leading to the bride's death, we should try. It is our imperial duty as well as our obligation to the poisoned bride and her mother.

(*The JUDGE paces again, then stops.*)

With respect to the other investigation, when Chao and Ma have completed the examination of the properties around the Bee residence, we should have a discussion about the case of the Reluctant Corpse. I am interested in what you each think about the circumstances of the crime.

TAO: We could send the notice for exhumation and then question the family of the deceased.

JUDGE DEE: Good idea. Inspector Hong, please deliver the notice of exhumation to the Registrar of Births and Deaths and tell Mother Bee and Widow Bee that I intend to interview them. I am willing to go to their residence but if they … prefer … they may come here to my office. Make it clear to them that this discussion is not optional. (*He looked up with a grim smile.*)

(*Lights fade to black and return after four beats.*)

ACT 2, SCENE 3

(*Two days later, the Bee residence, LOWER LEFT on stage. JUDGE DEE enters with INSPECTOR HONG and a female assistant. MOTHER BEE, WIDOW BEE are already seated.*)

MOTHER BEE (*nervously*): Welcome to our humble house, Your Honor. Please sit down and have some refreshments.

(*The JUDGE and his party sit; the WIDOW clears her throat.*)

WIDOW BEE: Your Honor, Mother Bee is too polite to tell you that your presence here is far from welcome. We have allowed this visit only because of your threats. Judges who abuse their authority and take advantage of defenseless women are a blot on the Imperial Court.

JUDGE DEE (*deliberately*): Your husband is dead, Widow Bee. By all accounts he was a good and hard-working man, someone of value to society ... You have not co-operated in any way with our investigation into his death.

WIDOW BEE: He died of natural causes!

JUDGE DEE (*stares at her coldly*): Your attitude and actions did not help to establish that. But despite what you have done and said, I am reasonably persuaded that he did not die of natural causes. He was murdered and we are here to arrest you, Widow Bee.

MOTHER BEE (*with cries of anguish*): Ai, how can that be?

WIDOW BEE: Mother, do not say anything. You will only give this wicked official satisfaction by acknowledging his power over us poor women.

MOTHER BEE (*starts as she recognizes the JUDGE. She says in amazement*): You are the same man who helped me with my bundles. You said you could cure my granddaughter!

WIDOW BEE: Ha! Even then he was plotting how to take advantage of you to possess me!

JUDGE DEE (*testily*): Don't flatter yourself Widow Bee! The Inspector and the Clerk of the Court here are witnesses to all that goes on in your house. But first we would like you to describe the evening of your husband's death.

(*The Widow maintains an angry and sullen silence.*)

JUDGE DEE: Really, Widow Bee, is this how you prove your innocence?

MOTHER BEE: Daughter …

WIDOW BEE (*reluctantly*): It was the night of the Dragon Boat Festival and we had dinner with some friends. After dinner, my husband complained of feeling sick. He started vomiting and said his stomach hurt.

JUDGE DEE: Did anyone else suffered from these symptoms?

WIDOW BEE: No one. But my daughter fell ill a few days later. She recovered but has lost her voice.

JUDGE DEE: And since then you have adopted the strictest rules of widowhood?

WIDOW BEE: Some people think it is old-fashioned, but I happen to believe in it.

JUDGE DEE: You never go out and in fact never receive visitors.

WIDOW BEE: That's right.

JUDGE DEE (*with a hint of exasperation*): I do not believe further interrogation would be helpful. (*Addresses Mother Bee*) Mother Bee, we are arresting your daughter-in-law. She is coming with us right now but she will need some plain clothes—very plain and simple clothes. Would you please get some for her? ... There will be a hearing of the evidence. You will have plenty of notice and may bring anyone to keep you company.

MOTHER BEE: Will I be able to bring my granddaughter?

JUDGE DEE (*gently*): How old is she?

MOTHER BEE: Six.

JUDGE DEE: She is too young for these proceedings, Mother Bee. But I promise I will come back soon with herbs to treat her... Perhaps you'd like to invite one of your friends ... or one of your son's friends to accompany you to the hearing?

(*MOTHER BEE sobs and nods as she leaves to get suitable clothes for her daughter-in-law.*)

JUDGE DEE: Widow Bee, we have exhumed your late husband's body.

WIDOW BEE (*outraged*): How dare you do that without our permission!

JUDGE DEE (*admiring and deploring the WIDOW's continued defiance*): Did I need your permission? Anyway, we were unable to determine what he had eaten that might have caused the symptoms you have described. (*Sits up straight in his chair.*) But the coroner found a long thin nail driven into the back of his head. Death would have occurred soon after this. (*Stands.*) Such a thing cannot have happened accidently and is certainly not the result, as you have said, of some illness. Do you have any idea how this could have happened?

(*WIDOW BEE looks at the JUDGE with angry silence.*)

JUDGE DEE: Are you acquainted with a young man named Su? (*Paces in small circle.*) How often have you met each other since your husband's death?

(*WIDOW BEE maintains her silence but her anger changes into sullenness.*)

JUDGE DEE: This would go much better for you if you would co-operate. (*Sighs and paces again.*) We will soon discover the truth regarding your actions since your husband's death, after we search your house thoroughly and question Young Su. ... I shall also return soon to administer herbs that will cure your daughter. (*He stops and says sadly.*) She might be able to help us by telling us what she has seen.

(*Lights now include a spot on WIDOW BEE whose cold stare turns to a panic-stricken look. All lights fade to black for four beats and come up on the next scene.*)

ACT 2, SCENE 4

(A few days later, in the house of Elder Hua, the Retired Prefect. JUDGE DEE is greeted by YOUNG HUA. Perhaps, the "action" can take place mostly in the LOWER LEFT portion of the stage.)

YOUNG HUA: Welcome, Your Honor.

JUDGE DEE: Thank you. I hoped to pay my respects to your illustrious father.

YOUNG HUA: He begs to be excused as he is not well. He told me to answer all your questions and show you around our humble house.

(He invites the Judge to sit before he himself also sits.)

JUDGE DEE: My belated condolences on the passing of your bride.

YOUNG HUA: Thank you, Your Honor. My father showed me your letter requesting his permission to visit and discuss that painful event. He says to tell you that he would expect nothing less from you than a full investigation … Your associate, Tao, has already made many inquiries here of the servants and no doubt has the names of all the guests as well.

JUDGE DEE *(amused)*: I hope she has not been too much trouble.

YOUNG HUA: Not at all. I learned something useful in hearing about your unusual investigator, although I have not actually talked to her. I gather you employ her and a couple of others with, er, similar backgrounds to assist in your work. Sounds like a brilliant idea. Studying for the exams taught me nothing about how to handle an investigation such as this.

JUDGE DEE (*teasing*): You do not believe that Confucius and the classics teach us how to think about mundane things like theft and death?

YOUNG HUA (*smiles*): I hope I adapt to that world as smoothly and swiftly as Your Honor has.

JUDGE DEE: Ah, you should save the pretty speeches for your future superiors ... What has Tao done?

YOUNG HUA: She has made friends with the servants and learned who were close to my bride and me on that day. There were two of them and, apart from the wedding feast, no one else served us. (*Fervently.*) The two have been my nurses and chief maids. I would trust them with my life.

JUDGE DEE: Did you spend any time separated from your bride?

YOUNG HUA (*shakes his head*): Not after the ceremonies.

JUDGE DEE: Did you share everything to eat or drink with your bride.

YOUNG HUA: Everything! ... Except ... Now I recall that my bride was thirsty and asked for some hot water just before we went to bed. I did not have any as I ... had plenty to drink during the banquet.

JUDGE DEE: Who served it to her?

YOUNG HUA: One of those two maids I told you about. Tao probably knows her name and may have spoken to her.

JUDGE DEE: Would the water have come from the kitchen?

YOUNG HUA: I suppose so, although I don't know that for a fact.

JUDGE DEE: Are you familiar with the kitchen?

YOUNG HUA (*shrugs his shoulders*): I must confess that I have not been in it for many years.

JUDGE DEE (*He rises*): Would you please do me a big favor?

YOUNG HUA: Of course.

JUDGE DEE (*Gesturing*): Would you please draw a diagram of your house—showing where the reception was, where the dinner was held, your bed-room, the kitchen and all adjacent rooms?

YOUNG HUA: I will send it to your office tomorrow… It may not be as good as the one that Tao has probably drawn (*with a laugh*).

JUDGE DEE (*smiles*): Ah, one diagram is good, two would be better. I hope you don't mind if, after reviewing the diagrams I have a few questions?

YOUNG HUA: Of course not. My father told me that he completely understands your motives and wished me to convey his compliments to you on taking your duties with such gravity. Would you like a tour of our house?

(*He rises and gestures around.*)

JUDGE DEE: I would like that very much ... By the way, I met your mother-in-law, Widow Lee, recently. She is grateful for your family's hospitality but believes it best for her to be on her own. She was most anxious that everyone understands she had done this of her own free will.

YOUNG HUA: Thank you for confirming that for me. I was distressed when we found her missing, although she left a note saying just that. Is she well?

JUDGE DEE: She is indeed, and she intends to pay you a visit soon to confirm all this in person. She is grateful, you know, for the hospitality of your family.

YOUNG HUA (*chokes back a sob*): My bride asked this of me and it seemed the most natural thing to do.

JUDGE DEE (*nodding*): We think this investigation is appropriate for memory of your bride.

(*Lights fade to black. After four beats, the lights come up for the next scene.*)

ACT 2, SCENE 5

(Two days later, JUDGE DEE is seated in his chambers LOWER RIGHT when TAO enters.)

JUDGE DEE: Welcome back, Tao. What do you have?

TAO: The servants were very co-operative.

JUDGE DEE (*He gestures Tao to a chair*): I would hope so after the Retired Prefect told them to answer your questions fully.

TAO (*surprised*): He did?

JUDGE DEE (*nods*): I learned this when I went to visit yesterday… it was somewhat embarrassing.

TAO: Well, I won't claim all the credit then—just half. How about that?

JUDGE DEE (*rolls his eyes*): Go on.

TAO: I believe, as I had thought, that the bride was poisoned, but I can't pin-point who did it. The servants who looked after the bridal couple are the two most trusted in the household. They had been Young Hua's nursemaids and are now his chief servants. All the servants say the bridal couple ate the same things as everyone else.

JUDGE DEE: Did anyone examine her body after she died?

TAO: Oh yes, your Honor. Her mother was there and thought her daughter might have been bitten. She and the two maids went over every inch of the body after the bride … and er…

JUDGE DEE: Yes, yes. So, if she had not been bitten by something poisonous, then she must have eaten or drunk something poisonous.

TAO: Well, Your Honor, she and her husband and their guests all ate and drank together.

JUDGE DEE: When they retired, did she eat or drink anything he did not?

TAO (*thoughtfully*): One of the maids waiting on them said the bride was thirsty and asked for some hot water.

JUDGE DEE (*nodding*): But the husband did not touch it, right?

TAO: That is so, Your Honor. I see you have confirmed this with Young Hua.

JUDGE DEE: We must work together on this, little sister. It is when we hear different things from the same people that we are nudged closer to the truth.

TAO (*shakes her head*): I don't think either of the maids could possibly have poisoned her, Your Honor.

JUDGE DEE: But where did the maid get the water from?

TAO: I see. Your Honor, she got it from the usual place.

JUDGE DEE: The kitchen?

(*TAO looks at the JUDGE for a moment, thinking.*)

TAO: No!

JUDGE DEE: No?

TAO: No. (*Shakes her head.*) Now I remember. She said that the large kettle was empty as the other servants had each taken away a portion for those they served. Ah (*straining to recall a half-forgotten conversation*), she got the water from a small open pot that was on a stove in the room just outside the kitchen!

JUDGE DEE (*pulling out a sheet of paper*): Show me on the diagram of the house. (*Pulling back the diagram for a moment.*) Do you have one of these also?

(*Tao smiles as she pulls a sheet of paper out of her pocket and waves it so that it unfolds. She and the JUDGE place them side by side on a small side table between them and look at each in turn.*)

TAO: Here. (Sh*e points to a spot on her map.*) It is not far from the bridal chamber.

JUDGE DEE: Yes, I was actually taken to that room... There was a funny smell, something moldy … and Young Hua said something about having the servants wash it thoroughly and burn some incense to get rid of the smell. Do you remember a smell in that room?

TAO: Now that you mention it, Your Honor, I did, and the maids who showed me around said something about how they had tried for months to get rid of that smell. (*Solemnly.*) One or two thought it had to do with the death of the bride, (*suggesting with body language that they had thought or mentioned something paranormal*) but most of them remembered the smell from before that unhappy event.

JUDGE DEE: Do you think you could go back and take another look around that room and at the way to and from that room to the bridal chamber? (*The JUDGE gives TAO a quizzical look.*)

TAO: I am sure I could, Your Honor. I burned no bridges the last time—at least none that I know of.

JUDGE DEE: Then please do so as soon as you can. Remember to look all around each room and don't forget to look UP as well.

TAO: What should I be looking for?

JUDGE DEE: Any source of poison … You're not testing me, are you?

TAO: Heaven forbid. I'll head for the Hua residence right now.

(*TAO exits as INSPECTOR HONG, MA, and CHAO enter.*)

INSPECTOR HONG: We had a fruitful search, Your Honor, although we could not find any records of the properties where the Bee family and their neighbors the Su family reside, that is, (*gestures at Ma*) until Young Ma here thought of asking to examine the files where *recent transfers* of title are kept.

MA: It turns out that the properties do not *now* belong to the Su family. They were *sold* to the Fan family over a year ago. That family moved in to the main part of the compound with a smaller house adjacent to theirs. The smaller house's where the Bee family has lived for many years... Um, there does appear to be a secret passageway between the main house and the smaller one.

JUDGE DEE (*with irritation at himself*): I should have remembered something so complicated.

MA: It happened just before your transfer here, Your Honor. But there is an interesting provision of the sale. Um, it specifies that the Fan family allow Young Su to keep an apartment in a wing of the main house.

JUDGE DEE (*surprised*): Really?

INSPECTOR HONG: Indeed, Your Honor, we thought the provision to be suspicious, but actually that all happened before he became acquainted with Widow Bee.

JUDGE DEE: How does he remembers the time so precisely?

CHAO: The property transaction was completed several months before the last Dragon Boat Festival. Young Su remembers that he first met Widow Bee about a month before the Festival... They were both in the marketplace and he had knocked her basket as he wandered about absent-mindedly looking for items his mother had requested that he buy for her. The Widow gave him a look that he says "ravished" him.

JUDGE DEE (*primly*): Hm. Well, the Dragon Boat Festival is an important one.

INSPECTOR HONG: Yes, it celebrates the memory of an upright minister.

MA (*reminiscing*): I remember it vaguely being about that but more for the special dumplings we had. Our village was not near any river or lake.

JUDGE DEE (*seizing the "teachable moment"*): The origins of the festival are very important. Nearly a thousand year ago, before China was united in an empire, it was divided into several kingdoms. The ruler of one of those saw that the Chin kingdom was going to succeed in conquering all the others and decided to enter into an alliance with the Chin. One of his ministers thought this would be a very bad idea and protested this alliance by committing suicide. (*Throws out his arms in a gesture.*) He threw himself into the river.

INSPECTOR HONG: The Dragon Boat Festival commemorates the faithfulness of this minister to the kingdom he served even though the Chin finally gave the Middle Kingdom its true form as a united Empire, all under Heaven. (*Shrugs.*) We Chinese believe a man does not have to be devoted to the winning side for his loyalty to be celebrated with reverence.

JUDGE DEE: But now it has provided a womanizing son of the gentry a way to track the progress of his affair.

CHAO: Not his fault, Your Honor, he did not know she was married. She certainly did, but it didn't stop her.

JUDGE DEE (*wearily*): I wonder if the world has gone mad—first Shao's woman and now this Widow.

CHAO (*tactfully*): Your Honor is the moralist, not me, but the situations are different—Shao's woman told him what she was like because he wanted to marry her. The woman was honest with him, giving him fair warning as it were. (*He shrugs.*) The Widow, on the other hand, seems to have out-grown the financial or social standing of her husband.

JUDGE DEE (*thoughtfully*): We can be quite sure that she did kill her husband because of the nail we found in his head during the exhumation. Are we sure now that this is WHY she did it?

INSPECTOR HONG: She might confess to it.

MA: We do know that the affair with Su began very soon after that chance meeting. Young Su told us that he met her at the market again and she asked if he lived in the Fan property. She told him that she had noticed him there and then announced she was his neighbor.

JUDGE DEE (*drily*): He might have noticed that his neighbor was a family with a child and a grandmother.

CHAO: He did. (*Speaking very carefully*): But she told him that the husband was often out at night, fishing the entire night. He says she asked if he could find a way to call on her secretly!

INSPECTOR HONG: That set him thinking and he remembered the secret passage-way from his childhood in the house…All very convenient!

MA: We found the passageway when we searched the Bee residence. It leads from a door very easily overlooked in the Bee residence to the Fan family ancestral shrine. That's probably where the Su family ancestral shrine had been. There is a trick panel that Young Su used for his visits.

JUDGE DEE (*grumpily, to himself*): No doubt designed and used by the father.

INSPECTOR HONG: The granddaughter and Su are also acquainted with each other. When I took her out for a walk in the market place after the herbal treatments Your Honor administered, she saw and greeted him. Su was delighted that she had regained her voice.

(*The BAILIFF enters.*)

BAILIFF: Pardon me, your Honor, a woman identifying herself as Mother Bee is here and wishes to speak.

JUDGE DEE: Did she ask for me?

BAILIFF: Actually, she asked to speak with the Inspector.

JUDGE DEE: You better go then, Inspector. (*Teasing,*) This is what you get for being nice to widows and children.

(*INSPECTOR HONG exits.*)

JUDGE DEE: What did Young Su think when Husband Bee died?

CHAO: He was assured that it had been a misadventure and said that after two or three months the Widow hinted that the two of them could soon … be together… openly. Su said he told her he didn't think it was proper to do so too quickly.

MA: Perhaps the Widow became impatient as the months went by and told Young Su during one of their tiffs that she had killed her husband in order to be free to be with him ... that might have frightened him.

CHAO: He claims now that he is filled with remorse that his selfish and immoral behavior had led to a man's death and that he no longer wants to have anything to do with the Widow. He said he wanted to break off their relationship.

JUDGE DEE: When did he tell the Widow?

MA: He says he has not done so yet… The Widow has her wiles.

JUDGE DEE (*drily*): He wants to leave his immoral ways, only not just now.

(*MOTHER BEE from OFF-STAGE*) Please tell the JUDGE, I mean no disrespect but I need to leave.

(*INSPECTOR HONG returns.*)

INSPECTOR HONG (*puzzled*): Mother Bee came to say she has had a discussion with her grand-daughter she wishes to report. The little girl mentioned meeting Young Su and told her grandmother he was glad to hear her talking again… Mother Bee says she did not know who her granddaughter was talking about and so the girl explained who Su is and when she had seen him… She apparently is a restless sleeper and would often get up to get a drink of water in the middle of the night… She often saw or met Young Su in the company of her mother.

JUDGE DEE (*rises to his feet, suddenly concerned about Mother Bee*): How did Mother Bee get here? We know she has trouble walking.

INSPECTOR HONG: A neighbor offered her a ride here in his cart and waited to take her back home. That's why she had to leave so quickly. Mother Bee says she regrets that she did not watch over her daughter-in-law more carefully.

JUDGE DEE (*turning his attention back to the case*): So, the Widow saw the need to silence her daughter and gave her some drug or herbs to make her mute. At least the solution did not entail another death. (*He shudders.*)

MA: Your Honor should be able to get a confession from the widow now. Young Su would also testify to the affair, which provides the motive. Her mother-in-law and daughter —

JUDGE DEE (*interrupting not rudely or consciously, but because his mind is racing ahead*): She is a strong-minded woman but I hope she has the good sense to know when she has lost—more than her husband—in her schemes. Inspector, would you like to get the confession from her? I think she is tired of seeing my face. Make sure you have both the female clerks … as well as the Jailer with you.

(*Addressing all the investigators, the JUDGE continued*):

Good work. Three capital cases solved in a month—you can all be proud.

(*All exit except the JUDGE who gets up to pace and stretch. The BAILIFF enters.*)

BAILIFF (*with a studiously blank face*): Your Honor has a visitor.

(*The BAILIFF exits as the IMPERIAL CENSOR enters in disguise. The JUDGE looks at him calmly. As soon as the CENSOR reveals his imperial insignia, the JUDGE drops to his right knee in a bow and brings his right fist over his heart in a salute.*)

JUDGE DEE: Your Excellency.

IMPERIAL CENSOR: Your Honor, please get up. (*JUDGE DEE stands up.*) You have probably guessed at the identity of the stranger in your courtroom.

66

JUDGE DEE: I am honored by your visit.

IMPERIAL CENSOR (*nods*): You are a brave and inspired servant of the Empire.

JUDGE DEE (*smiles*): Would it be appropriate to offer Your Excellency some tea?

IMPERIAL CENSOR (*also smiles*): It is appropriate and would be much appreciated... I waited twenty years for this tea-drinking fad to pass ... It didn't and so a few months ago I decided I would try it.

JUDGE DEE: Your Excellency does not rush to try out new fashions?

IMPERIAL CENSOR: I don't think so. In fact, I am convinced that going through our examination hell—just between the two of us, you understand—has beaten that inclination out of every candidate ... When I discovered that the tea drinking was not just a passing fad, I decided to try it ... I rather like some versions of tea.

(*The JUDGE claps twice; a clerk enters.*)

JUDGE DEE: You know where the tea is? (*The clerk nods.*) Please, bring us some.

(*The clerk leaves. The Judge gestures to two chairs and the Censor sits followed by the Judge.*)

IMPERIAL CENSOR (*clears his throat*): The Imperial Court has taken note of your efforts to deal with the crimes at your previous position and here at your current one ... There are still those at the Court who remember your grandfather, the Imperial Minister, and many more your father the Illustrious Prefect ... Some of your cases, however, are thought to be somewhat unorthodox, and the rumors concerning the kind of men, and even a ... woman, you have employed as your investigators have raised more eyebrows. Hence it was decreed that I should come and observe.

(The clerk enters with steaming tea in two cups on a tray for the two men and leaves after setting the tray on a small side table between the two men.)

JUDGE DEE: There were times when the classics and consultation with my fellow members in the Imperial Service shed no light and I had to *(shrugs)* … improvise. I have much to learn and would be grateful for guidance.

IMPERIAL CENSOR: You came close to scandal with the accusations of Widow Bee. *(The CENSOR grimaced and wrinkled his nose.)* Elder Hua, the Retired Prefect was initially much annoyed that you proceeded to investigate the death of his daughter-in-law after he had pronounced her death a misadventure. But he is an upright man and soon realized that you, not he, would be held responsible for any wrong-doing that is undetected or unpunished.

JUDGE DEE: The Widow was … is a strong-willed person and was determined to have her way. But I believe we have uncovered evidence that she committed the murder and also her motive for doing so. Inspector Hong is about to confront her with what we know and the witnesses we can bring against her; he should have her confession soon.

IMPERIAL CENSOR *(earnestly)*: That is good … Even the false accusations of a person of dubious morality like the Widow *(with emphasis)* can taint the reputation of an upright servant of the Imperial Court.

JUDGE DEE *(nods to signify his agreement, and then changes the subject)*: I am pleased to hear that Honored Elder Hua does not hold a grudge. It was a horrible death that his daughter-in-law suffered and for her sake as well as that of her mother I felt it necessary to pursue the truth.

IMPERIAL CENSOR (*with a slight hesitation*): Ye-es.

JUDGE DEE (*calmly and deliberately*): If the death had been that of Young Hua the groom, I have no doubt that there would have been an inquiry. (*He says the following with great intensity.*) If the death had been that of the Illustrious Prefect himself, I am certain that the imperial authorities would have moved heaven and earth to uncover the truth.

(*The IMPERIAL CENSOR remains silent but becomes thoughtful.*)

JUDGE DEE (*firmly*): A young woman of humble birth is not, Your Excellency, any less a subject of his imperial majesty. She deserves no less of our effort to find the truth of her unfortunate death.

(*Both men reached for their tea and drank in solemn silence.*)

IMPERIAL CENSOR (*with relish*): This tea is excellent, "Tie-guan-yin" is it not?

JUDGE DEE: Yes, I don't understand why the Fujianese bother to produce anything else… I suppose some teas are not so flavorful and need "enhancements."

IMPERIAL CENSOR: Do not be hasty, Your Honor. I have heard of a tea flavored with jasmine flowers that is quite popular at the Imperial Court. We have also received reports that along the Silk Road, various tribes add other herbs or spices to their tea which they buy from us. Is it not said, the public is always right?

JUDGE DEE: I will try to keep an open mind on this subject … although I am inclined to stop looking for variations when I have found something I like.

IMPERIAL CENSOR (*getting up*): Well, Your Honor, I look forward to the resolution of your investigations. Three cases involving death in one month—your reputation shall need no enhancements after this.

JUDGE DEE (*gets to his feet also*): Your Excellency is too kind.

(*Lights fade to black; four beats and then they come up for the next scene.*)

ACT 2, SCENE 6

(*JUDGE DEE'S Courtroom. Whole Cast, except JUDGE DEE and the Bee girl, is on stage and seated.*)

BAILIFF: The Court of the Honorable Judge Dee is now in session. All rise!

(*JUDGE DEE enters and sits, signaling that all present may also sit.*)

JUDGE DEE: In the Case of the Double Homicide, the guilty person has been found and has confessed. Young Shao, please stand.

(*SHAO stands up in his place.*)

JUDGE DEE: For killing two men, one a fellow tradesman and the other an old farmer who simply happened to be passing by, and for stealing a cart of silk goods belonging to your fellow tradesman, I hereby sentence you to death. You will be executed as soon as this verdict and sentence have been reviewed and confirmed in accordance with Imperial law. This sentence and your confession have been sent to the Imperial Court. Do you wish to add anything?

SHAO (*with great emotion*): It is a terrible thing to kill even one man, let alone two. I know this. I just don't know what came over me. Anything I might say would be a shameful excuse, I deserve to die.

(*The JAILER leads SHAO, who looks like a man without hope, away. JAILER returns quietly as the Judge is speaking.*)

JUDGE DEE: In the case of the Reluctant Corpse, we have identified this as a homicide that previously was reported as a death

71

through natural causes. The guilty person has been found and has confessed. Widow Bee, please rise.

(WIDOW BEE stands up in her place. Her mother-in-law MOTHER BEE stifles a sob.)

JUDGE DEE: Widow Bee, you have been accused of murdering your husband and of filing false testimony that his death was due to natural causes. Confronted by various witnesses you have reluctantly confessed to this crime. You have also willfully drugged your daughter in order to deprive her of speech that might reveal your immoral behavior. The sentence for your crime is death. You will be executed as soon as this verdict and sentence have been reviewed and confirmed in accordance with Imperial law. This sentence and your confession have been sent to the Imperial Court. Do you have anything you wish to say?

WIDOW BEE *(conscience-stricken but composed)*: My husband, daughter, and mother-in-law have given me nothing but their love. In return I have killed my husband and tried to silence my daughter. Mother Bee, I ask for your forgiveness even though I do not deserve it. Please look after your grand-daughter for your son's sake and explain if you can to her that, in my own way, I loved her too.

(The JAILER leads the WIDOW out.)

JUDGE DEE: In the case of the Poisoned Bride, Illustrious Elder Hua, a Retired Prefect, pronounced that his daughter-in-law died through an act of fate. In the interest of maintaining the faith between the Imperial Court and its citizens, however, this Court has pursued its investigation independently but with the generous accommodation of the illustrious prefect, since the bride died in his household. We now have certain findings that should be reported. Investigator Tao, please make your report.

72

(*TAO rises. The audience murmurs at seeing a woman as investigator.*)

TAO: The circumstances of the Bride's death clearly pointed to death by poisoning. But we could not find anyone with the motive or the opportunity to have committed such an act. Directed by the Judge, and with the liberal permission of the Hua family...

(*TAO bows in the direction of YOUNG HUA and continues*):

I therefore examined the premises. I discovered that when the victim asked for some hot water just before retiring, the maid brought her a cup, not from the usual large kettle in the kitchen as there was no water left in it, but from a small open pot on a stove in the adjacent room. I examined this room and found that there is a nest of vipers under the eaves of the roof, directly above the pot.

(*The audience in the Courtroom murmurs loudly but is silenced by a hand raised by the JUDGE.*) It is my belief that some poison from a viper's fang dripped into the pot and that the bride was thus poisoned.

JUDGE DEE: Thank you, Investigator Tao. This court concurs with the verdict pronounced earlier by Elder Hua of death by misadventure. We recommend now that the Hua family consults the temple authorities and arranges to have the appropriate rites and ceremonies performed. Does anyone have anything to add to this sad story?

IMPERIAL CENSOR (*rises and steps forward to speak*): With your indulgence, Your Honor, allow me to say that the Illustrious Prefect Hua is grateful to you for continuing your investigation into the death of his daughter-in-law—for bringing peace to the hearts of all who loved her, and for exhibiting the best of Imperial concern and service to the people of the Middle Kingdom.

JUDGE DEE: Thank you, Your Excellency. Thank you all for your attendance. Court is adjourned.

(*Lights fade slowly as the BAILIFF cries out*)

BAILIFF: The Court of the Honorable JUDGE DEE is now adjourned. All rise!

(*Lights fade slowly as the courtroom empties. Two spots come on to single out JUDGE DEE and the IMPERIAL CENSOR. The JUDGE drops to his right knee and raises his right fist to his heart. The CENSOR places his right fist against the open palm of his left hand and gives a slight bow. Lights and spots fade quickly to black.*)

END

NOTES

In 1949, Robert van Gulik published *The Celebrated Cases of Judge Dee*. He based this on an eighteenth-century Chinese manuscript. "Detective novels" featuring judges from history abound in China and some were even more popular there than those revolving around the doings of Judge Dee. I have chosen to adapt *The Celebrated Cases* for *The Ingenious Judge Dee, a Play* because these stories initiated the whole endeavor in English.

Van Gulik published more than a dozen other stories featuring Judge Dee. Other authors of Judge Dee stories include Frédéric Lenormand, Zhu Xiao Di, and Sven Roussel, but we owe the popularity of these "cozy mysteries" in English primarily to van Gulik. I have tried to preserve this cozy tone in this play.

The Ingenious Judge Dee is set in 7th century China as a nod to the historical Judge Dee, but I have tried to write in a contemporary English idiom while giving it the tone of a rural and pre-modern setting. Writers of historical fiction have to resolve how to render twelfth century France or sixteenth century Persian or seventh century Chinese in modern day English. We struggle with the question that, even if the author does hit upon a suitable tone or voice for sixteenth century Persia, how would others, readers especially, know this?

There actually was a Tang imperial official named Dee, although he was not a judge. His full name in pinyin was Di Renjie and we know very little about him though we do know that he died in 700 A.D. Di served in the Imperial Civil Service starting as "magistrate," a position akin to that of the district officers who served in the British Empire in the "colonies." Such servants of the state advanced with increases to the territory over which they had authority, say, from one of the fifteen hundred counties to one of the twenty provinces of China. Like fathers over their households, Roman paterfamilias, or the emperor over the empire, they were judge and jury, investigator and prosecutor, with the power of life and death.

Fans of modern "police procedural" dramas must be cautioned against judging the action in this play with concepts like Miranda rights and illegal searches. Remember, Judge Dee belongs to a different country in a different century.

Perhaps this play will be performed and provide the occasion for all who enjoy reading the Judge Dee stories an opportunity to discuss their experience and enjoyment. Inquiries regarding performance rights may be sent to tjoa.books@gmail.com.

First, a note on the **Dragon Boat Festival.** This has traditionally been celebrated on the 5th day of the 5th month of the soli-lunar year. Hence the holiday is often referred to as the "double fifth." In 2008, the People's Republic of China made it (finally) a public holiday. It is celebrated in many places where Chinese live with small pyramid-shaped "dumplings" made with sticky rice and a variety of fillings—each wrapped in bamboo leaves and tied with twine. This is tricky to make as rice expands as it is cooked and the preparer must anticipate how much room to leave in the pre-tied package of bamboo leaves before the cooking. The celebrations frequently include Dragon Boat races, hence the other name of the festival. These can be quite spectacular with a suitable body of water (e.g., in Hong Kong).

Legend has it that the holiday honors the suicide of a statesman (in the 3rd century B.C.) who protested the alliance of his home state with the Qin, which eventually unified China. Thus, he was on the wrong side of history. His protest was accomplished by jumping from a bridge into a river. The boats and the dumplings represent the attempts the people made to divert the fish of the rivers or seas from nibbling on his body.

Second, something should be said about tea-drinking during the seventh century. Although tea was known very early in Chinese history (1st century B. C. or A. D.), it was not commonly or popularly drunk until the 8th century A.D. when the *Classic of Tea* was written and published (by Lu Yu in 780). During the lifetime of the historical Judge Dee therefore, it was probably not the common drink that it is today. The proper way to serve tea did not become the "tea ceremony" in Chinese etiquette until the 11th century (and thereafter in Japan).

Tie-guan-yin, pronounced ti'eh-gwan-yin meaning Iron Guanyin (Goddess of Mercy) is a particularly fine oolong originally from Fujian province but now grown in many places, rather-like "Cuban" tobacco grown from "Cuban seed" planted in other countries—with analogous results. Oolong, black (actually red) and green teas are primarily differentiated by differences in the curing/manufacturing process.

Unique among the black teas is pu-er, which is fermented and aged; it is an acquired taste. Jasmine tea is one of many examples of tea with flavor enhancements. Sometimes the enhancement was fortuitous, as in the case of lapsang souchong, a black tea that had for some forgotten reason to be dried in a hurry and was thus processed with the aid of fire hastily made with tarry pine logs.

Finally, I have modified the confusing forms of address the Chinese used traditionally. Often a person's name is accompanied by a title such as Illustrious Prefect Hua or a family designation like Mother

Bee and Widow Lee. Elder and Young so-an-so are much like senior and junior in English.

EXCERPT FROM THE BATTLE OF CHIBI

Long ago, along a stretch of a river deep and wide but far away from the consciousness or imagination of anyone outside All under Heaven (China), a battle was fought that determined the unity of the empire for the next four hundred years. It was there along the Yangzi that Liu Bei, the Loyalist, and Zhou Yu, commander in chief of Wu, the kingdom established by the most successful of the Chinese warlords, defeated Cao Cao, the Usurper. In defeating Cao's huge army and armada, Bei and Yu established Shu and Wu as powers together with Cao's Wei that would divide China into the Three Kingdoms.

The south bank of that stretch of river was called Chibi, Red Cliffs, and that name was given to the battle. Cao was forced to flee northwards back to his base; he regrouped his forces and, by virtue of holding the last Han Emperor hostage and of having the largest body of men in arms, remained the "First Man" of China, but he was never again able to threaten South China.

The *Romance of the Three Kingdoms* asserts in its very first chapter the Chinese view of history—not as a linear progression from primitive to developed (first-world status), but as an alternation between the unity of the Chinese Empire and political chaos, "disunity." It was a major achievement of Zhuge Liang to persuade his contemporaries that China could exist as a triangular balance of power—Loyalists, Usurpers and Wu/Jiangdong. Thus, after four hundred years of imperial unity under the Han dynasty, China came to be ruled by the Three Kingdoms. These kingdoms lasted only eighty years that with the three centuries that followed (before the establishment of a unified China by the Sui and Tang dynasties) became known as the Age of Fragmentation.

The *Romance* and hence this work are not merely about the military actions or political considerations of that era, but also about values. Perhaps the most crucial question was the implication for loyal subjects when Fate appears to have determined that a dynasty should end. (By the Ming dynasty, this was codified and thus resolved, but the Romance reflects the uncertain tension before such a resolution.) For many intellectuals, this conflict prompted a desire for the "contemplative life," reflecting perhaps an escapist yearning, perhaps the quietist aspect of Daoist thought. This preference is mixed with a sense of fatalism. Zhuge Liang is unafraid when he is in Wu/Jiangdong because the end of his life has been decreed by Fate--but he also planned meticulously for his final escape from Wu on board a boat that he orders a month in advance.

To tell of his many stratagems is to learn that, for Liang, not everything has been written in the Book of Fate or if it had, there was still the possibility that with enough effort and the right angle of vision, one might change the course of Fate. Liang's vision was to see China neither as an empire nor in chaos, as enunciated in the opening paragraph of the *Romance*; he believed that it could be ruled by three kingdoms and for a while he was successful. Perhaps he dared to think that this would enable him and "All under Heaven" to escape "Fate." To achieve this, however, he "coughed up his life's blood."

Part of the price to pay was a continued battle of wits between Liang and Zhou Yu of Jiangdong. This battle was itself a continuation of the vendetta between the two regions since Sun Jian, the patriarch of Jiangdong, was confronted by Liu Biao, Bei's kinsman and protector while he ruled Jingzhou; all retold in this volume. After

80

Biao's death, the dispute became one over territory—Jingzhou, which the Wu kingdom of Jiangdong regarded as an extension of its realm. The vendetta did not end with the death of Zhou Yu although this retelling of the Romance does, closing with Yu's funeral at which Liang mourns with a moving eulogy

From the Back Cover of the Battle of Chibi

"Fascinating insight into a whole new world of thought."

Hasan S. Padamsee, Professor of Physics, Cornell, NY.

"Lively and entertaining translation of a Chinese classic that deserves a wide audience."

Beryl S. Slocum, Salve Regina University, RI.

"Excellent translation, faithful to the spirit of the Romance as I recall from reading it many times (in Korean)."

Seung-il Shin, formerly Professor of Genetics, Albert Einstein College of Medicine, NY.

"Opens new vistas of fascinating history and thought."

Susan Wilson, Sierra College Library, CA.

See listings, http://sleepingdragonbooks.com/?page_id=82

EXCERPT FROM Agamemnon Must Die

PROLOGUE: IPHIGENIA

(Before the ships sail for Troy)

For three weeks this ominous summer in Greece, the winds have gusted and moaned, the seas have roiled and the skies have remained dark, baleful and gloomy. It was this doom-laden murkiness that unsettled and unmanned those gathered to sail their thousand ships. Thus, uncertain of his hold over the many half-hearted chieftains who had brought their men and ships on this quest, Agamemnon chose to offer up his lithesome daughter—bright-eyed, dark haired, and merry as the whistling larks of the air, Iphigenia—as the human sacrifice demanded by the gods. He had not expected any other chief to volunteer a virgin daughter when the oracle had made known the mind of the gods. With supplies running as low as the morale of the men, he ordered his daughter, bound and gagged, to be brought before him and he himself performed the sacrifice.

A wild shriek pierced the gloom. Her mother's cry, such a sound of love, loss, and anguish as had never before been heard, pierced the heart of every man there as Iphigenia bled quickly to her death. The shriek, the cry, now became a low moan as Clytemnestra threw herself beside the lifeless body of her child, who could have looked forward to years of play and young love, and (thought the queen, her mother) the many delicious decisions and rueful revisions she would now never make or unmake. This thought ignited the queen's anger and her moan shaped itself into a growl and then to a full-throated, guttural howl.

It seemed as if the sound reached through her loins into the depths of the earth to commune with Persephone, another doomed victim of male willfulness, and then ascended to reverberate in her womb. It resonated in the belly that bore her firstborn and in her chest to which she had clutched her baby to suckle with her milk-heavy breasts. From earth through mother, the wail rose to the skies without a quiver. It was utterly without hope, achingly and piercingly full of frustration and fury.

Agamemnon's lust stirred at the sight of Clytemnestra's breasts beneath her loose robe, but then embarrassed, he ordered the fleet to set sail immediately.

The mother's caterwaul continued. She howled in grief and longing for the life that was now gone. She raged against her husband's implacable drive to lead the Greeks against the Trojans, she stormed in anger, anguish and resentful futility until she was the only one left on the beach in Aulis, whence the fleet sailed for Troy.

At the ritual slaughter of her daughter, the storm clouds had instantly dispersed and Clytemnestra now walked back to the encampment where her husband and his troops had gathered in the typically brilliant sunshine of a summer day in Greece. She would not forgive or forget this moment. The salty tang of the spray from the waves refreshed her even as they smelled like the tears now drying from her cheeks. No one of the remnant left looked at her as she slouched her grim way to join them for the journey back to Mycenae. One elder, Aristides, more sympathetic than the others, roused himself to face her.

"My lady."

"Yes, councilor."

"Mourn your daughter on the journey to Mycenae, for when we arrive, you must rule."

From the Author of *Agamemnon Must Die*

Towards the end of the 13th century B.C., the "mother of all wars" for the millennium, the Trojan War is over. After ten years, Agamemnon of Mycenae who had led the Greeks on that epic battle has returned. All his people want is for their lives to return to normal.

But the gods have unfinished items on their agenda. In the middle of the 5th century B. C., Aeschylus wrote the Oresteia, a trilogy of plays, to give meaning to these memories. It was required reading for all classics major, but I didn't "get it" despite wrestling with a dozen or so translations.

This therefore is my retelling.

An early reader commented:

Agamemnon Must Die is a superbly-written retelling of the tale. The author combines verse with narrative in an effective way for 21st Century audiences.

Piper Templeton, author of Rain Clouds and Waterfalls.

View book listing

Contents

THE AUTHOR

Hock G. Tjoa was born in Singapore to Chinese parents. He studied history at Brandeis and Harvard and taught European history and Asian political thought at the University of Malaya in Kuala Lumpur. He is married and lives with his family in the Sierra Nevada foothills of California.

In 2010, he published *The Battle of Chibi*, selections translated from "The Romance of the Three Kingdoms" (one of four great "Ming" novels). In 2011, he adapted Lao She's "Tea House," Mandarin original dated 1953, publishing it as *Heaven is High and the Emperor Far Away, a Play*. Both are part of his goal to contribute to a wider and greater understanding of China and Asia.

Hock published *The Chinese Spymaster (volume 1: Operation Kashgar)* in 2013 and *Agamemnon Must Die, a retelling of Aeschylus' Oresteia* as well as *The Ingenious Judge Dee* in 2014 and *The Ninja and the Diplomat*, volume 2 of The Chinese Spymaster, in September 2015.

The Author's blog is

hockgtjoa.blogspot.com

His Amazon Author's page is

http://www.amazon.com/Hock-Guan-Tjoa/e/B001HPMVZY/

His Goodreads Author Profile is

http://www.goodreads.com/author/show/4537067.Hock_G_Tjoa

He tweets very occasionally and can be reached via Twitter @hgtjoa

His website is still under construction though portions are ready at www.sleepingdragonbooks.com.

His email address is tjoa.books@gmail.com

62181446R00059